For Your Garden

PATHS AND WALKWAYS

For Your Garden

PATHS AND WALKWAYS

DARIA PRICE BOWMAN

FRIEDMAN/FAIRFAX
PUBLISHERS

A FRIEDMAN/FAIRFAX BOOK

© 1999 by Michael Friedman Publishing Group, Inc.

Library of Congress Cataloging-in-Publication Data

Bowman, Daria Price.
        Paths and walkways / Daria Price Bowman.
                    p.   cm.
        Includes index.
        ISBN 1-56799-482-2
        1. Garden walks—Design and construction—Amateur's manuals.
        2. Landscape gardening—Amateurs' manuals.   I. Title.   II. Series.
        TH4970.B68 1997
        712—dc21   97-13134

Editor: Susan Lauzau
Art Director: Jeff Batzli
Designer: Jennifer Markson
Photography Editor: Wendy Missan
Production Manager: Camille Lee

Color separations by Fine Arts Repro House Co., Ltd.
Printed in Hong Kong by Midas Printing Limited.

3 5 7 9 10 8 6 4

For bulk purchases and special sales, please contact:
Friedman/Fairfax Publishers
Attention: Sales Department
15 West 26th Street
New York, New York 10010
212/685-6610 FAX 212/685-1307

Visit our website:
http://www.metrobooks.com

Table of Contents

INTRODUCTION

Gertrude Jekyll, one of the garden world's most revered designers, wrote in 1908 of the paths at Munstead Wood, her home in Surrey: "Five woodland walks pass upward through the trees; every one has its own character, while the details change during its progress—never abruptly, but in leisurely sequence; as if inviting the quiet stroller to stop a moment to enjoy some little woodland suavity, and then gently enticing him to go further, with agreeable anticipation of what might come next."

Miss Jekyll's woodland paths do all that garden paths should. They lead the visitor from one place to another, all the while traveling from one beautiful vista to another or suggesting special places to pause. And Jekyll's paths offer "agreeable anticipation"—the sense of mystery and surprise that the best gardeners strive to create in their gardens.

Just as each of the five paths at Munstead Wood has its own character, so do the paths and walkways designed and built by experienced gardeners and enthusiastic novices the world over.

Throughout the history of gardening, paths and walkways have played a vital role. The pharaohs of ancient Egypt created geometric gardens within an elaborate framework of intersecting paths. In ancient Rome, flower beds were surrounded by mosaic-studded paths, while the heaven-on-earth gardens of early Islam often featured stone walkways flanking pools and canals.

In medieval Europe, monks tended "physick" gardens, in which they grew medicinal herbs in neat rows separated by narrow walkways. Later gardens built for the owners of palaces and grand manor houses used formal designs that relied heavily on parterre formations of geometric beds flanked by brick or gravel paths. Grand French chateaux like Versailles and Vaux-le-Vicomte, the Medicis' Italian villas, and English palaces and estates on the order of Hampton Court featured extraordinary formal gardens with intricate designs of flower beds and paths. By the eighteenth century, a more romantic view of landscaping became fashionable, and with it came the notion of meandering paths through a naturalistic landscape.

And while complex gardening themes were carried out on a grand scale by the very rich, farmers and villagers tended their own modest backyard gardens. In these small spaces—where fruits, vegetables, and herbs were grown for the table—paths and walkways existed as functional elements of the garden.

Today, gardeners have distilled the history of their craft, and use the elements they like most and those that fit their needs. In a grand garden, a wide and perfectly manicured grass lawn serves as a dividing path between lushly planted herbaceous borders, an arrangement beloved by two hundred years of English gardeners.

Simple stepping stones mark the way through a tumble of flowers in a country cottage garden, following yet another centuries-old tradition. In a woodland garden, an unobtrusive trail among naturalized daffodils and bluebells becomes more distinct with a thick layer of pine bark mulch.

Though the challenges of modern urban and suburban living could not even have been imagined when the first paths were created, twentieth-century gardeners have adapted the age-old principles of path-making to their own needs. Concrete pavers set right into the lawn run from back door to garage in a suburban backyard, protecting the turf from heavy use, while outlining the boundaries of a vegetable garden.

OPPOSITE: The extraordinary visual delights of glowing yellow laburnum panicles and the purple lollipop heads of alliums below are firmly anchored by the skillfully designed path and columnar focal point. The path's rigid straight lines are further strengthened by the combination of smooth stone edging that encloses the highly textured, rounded cobbles of the central path.

The act of walking down a garden path, too, is as old and revered as gardening itself. Sometimes it is merely the infinitely practical act of moving from one part of the garden to another. At others times, the movements are simply the back and forth of a busy gardener as he or she tends to the beds along the path. There are yet other moments when nothing is more romantic than a stroll along a woodland path hand-in-hand with the one you love.

In the following pages, we will see how gardeners have used stones and bricks, wood and earth in a myriad of styles and interpretations to create their garden paths and walkways. Some have reached into the past for inspiration, while others looked only to their own imaginations. There are exquisitely elaborate paths and others that are simply functional—but all enhance the beauty of their gardens, add mystery and surprise with curves and turns, define spaces, or call attention to special plantings or ornaments. There is also a garden style to suit every taste, ranging from stately formal gardens to tiny sideyard borders to wildflower meadows. And, of course, no matter what their material, design, or milieu, these paths take the gardener from here to there.

RIGHT: Irregular, broken stones are pieced together like a jigsaw puzzle in this stunning backyard garden. On either side of the narrow walk, which leads to a venerable purple beech at the rear, are the varied colors and textures of perennials, groundcovers, and evergreen and deciduous shrubs.

OPPOSITE: A vividly painted wooden bridge does more than keep one's feet dry when crossing a stream. Here, the vibrant color becomes a foil for the velvety petals of lavender Siberian iris. The bridge also draws the viewer's eyes away and across to another part of the garden, where other sights will unfold when the irises have faded. The strong lines and color of the bridge also provide visual interest in winter, when little color remains in the surrounding garden.

ABOVE: A narrow, basketweave brick path winds its way past a white and silver border of irises, stocks, lavender, and artemisia. Paths like this one serve as a protective buffer for mowing, as well as a visual transition between the lawn and the planting bed.

RIGHT: Amid the tumble of color in the yellow garden at Wollerton Old Hall in Shropshire, an opening in a brick wall beckons visitors to explore the cooler recesses of the garden beyond the iron gate. The transition from gravel path to geometric cut stone walkway reinforces the visual impact of the passage from the exuberant perennial border to a more sedate design.

ABOVE: The wooden edging of this pea gravel path is all but obscured by the tumble of 'Rose du Mai' dianthus, catmint, and other sprawling plants. Order is maintained in this casual tangle of blooms typical of a cottage garden by intersecting paths and by the positioning of carefully clipped boxwood blocks. The willow-leafed pear at the intersection adds vertical interest to a complex and pleasing design.

OPPOSITE: The gentle, winding curves of a pebble path repeat the rounded forms of azaleas, boxwood, and mounds of lilyturf (*Liriope* spp.), and encourage the visitor to walk further. In this garden, the dark green of the groundcover plants is not permitted to disrupt the clean lines of the path by spilling onto the walkway. Though this is a woodland garden, its manicured appearance speaks of vigilant and careful upkeep.

ABOVE: Irregularly shaped beds of lavender, Russian sage, perennial geraniums, and other tightly mounded plants form islands in the buff-colored gravel paths. At the center of this tapestry garden is the vibrant green of a chamomile lawn anchored with a graceful ornament.

OPPOSITE: The hard lines of a brick path are softened by a well-established planting of deep purple irises that exuberantly oversteps the confines of a bed and encroaches on the walkway. Hardy geraniums, lady's mantle, catmint, daylilies, lamb's ears, and other clump-forming or sprawling varieties will produce a similar informal effect.

ABOVE: Strips of mowed meadow become country lanes in this tranquil orchard. The simplest of all paths, the mowed trail can be re-created year after year, with the lane's direction dictated by whim or necessity.

RIGHT: A pair of luxuriant beds densely planted with delphiniums, lady's mantle, roses, and wallflowers are divided by a wide grass path. The path originates at an axis marked by rose-covered arches and ends with a gate leading to a meadow beyond. Grass paths used in this manner should be meticulously maintained so as not to detract from the other elements in the garden.

ABOVE: A well-worn grass path lies within the cool recesses of a hornbeam hedge. Paths like this straight allée usually lead directly to a vista or a destination. In this case, the enclosed path leads the eye as well as the foot to the gleaming white door of a charming summer house.

LEFT: Mat-forming groundcovers, natural clusters of chives, yarrow, and other herbs, informal groups of terra-cotta pots, and a lily-pad covered pond belie the formality of this garden's geometric brick paths. Were this garden designed with precise box edging, symmetrical plantings, and smart topiary standards at the corners, its mood would be transformed from comfortably casual to formal and elegant.

Chapter One

DOWN THE GARDEN PATH

A path may be no more than a utilitarian route from one important site to another, say, from the door to the mailbox. Or perhaps it's a deliberate detour through a particularly picturesque part of the garden or a carefully laid out series of intersecting paths built on a rigid axis. A path might also be a wandering trail designed for romantic walks.

As paths become more intricate and elaborate, so does the design process. An uncomplicated dirt track through the woods may evolve over time into a woodland trail distinguished by stepping stones to mark the way. A kitchen garden may begin with nothing more than a layer of straw forming a footway between the rows, but may eventually adopt a more formal demeanor when brick pavers replace the straw.

Often, in suburban backyards or large rural properties, vast expanses of lawn evolve into broad swaths of mixed beds or perennial borders, with the remaining lawn reassigned to the role of a grassy path between the beds.

Then there are the existing paths from front yard to back or from terrace to garden shed that in an earlier time were constructed of serviceable but not terribly attractive cement. These everyday walkways are given a new life as pretty garden paths when repaved with bricks, flagstones, or a thick layer of pea gravel.

Other garden paths are designed and laid out before the soil is tilled or the plants sown. Designers prepare detailed plans with paths drawn on a grid forming an east-west or north-south axis, thus creating long-range vistas. Even more important, a well thought-out walkway will lend "bones," or structure, to the garden as a whole.

The most successful paths and walkways—the ones that entice the visitor into the garden or further into a meadow, the ones that elicit admiring nods or even a little gasp of pleasure—are those that truly fit the spaces they fill. The materials—stone, tile, brick, wood, or grass—and the form, whether intersecting avenues or curving footpaths, must complement the theme of the garden and enhance the nature of the space. So, too, must the length of the path—from a short stretch connecting deck and driveway to a long and meandering woodland walk—suit its ultimate purpose.

That is not to say that all cottage gardens should have rambling gravel paths and every pair of herbaceous borders simply must be divided by a grassy lane. Though certain conventions are often adopted by gardeners, the character of the garden and its paths and walkways should be a reflection of the tastes, talents, and expectations of the people who live there, of those who walk the paths.

OPPOSITE: A grass path seems to disappear into the darkness of the woods, only to reappear in a speck of light at the far end. Standing guard are a group of trimmed hornbeams pruned as standards. An ornamental urn atop a marble plinth further accentuates the path's mysterious destination. In this garden, the path is a seamless extension of the lawn. Grass paths should be made wide enough to accommodate lawn mowers easily.

ABOVE, LEFT: Narrow ribbons of gravel form diagonal paths in an intimate, enclosed garden. The slender walkways form the outlines of formal triangular planting beds edged with tiny boxwood hedges and punctuated with boxwood cones.

ABOVE, RIGHT: A pair of towering trees separated by a gate marks the transition from garden to meadow. The grass path continues beyond the gate and becomes a wilder version of itself. Within the garden framework, the path is a foil to an extensive mixed woodland border of azaleas, rhododendrons, ferns, cotoneaster, and lamb's ears.

OPPOSITE: A high curved brick wall encloses a large and extravagantly planted garden. Here, a gravel path wide enough for two follows the curve of the wall while creating a visual break between a hot color border of reds and oranges and the cooler tones of purples and lavender. Though the path is edged with boards, the unrestrained plants tumble into the walkway, blurring the edges and creating a wavy pattern of their own.

ABOVE: Pairs of weathered planks form a bridge across a pond edged with hostas, ferns, irises, and other moisture-loving plants. The staggered positioning of the planks and the simplicity of their vertical supports suggest an oriental theme in this expansive water garden.

RIGHT: A light rain adds a sheen to the arched wooden slats of a simple bridge. The bridge connects two parts of a gravel path that travels through a mature garden of large azaleas, Japanese maples, ferns, groundcovers, and perennials. Large stones, artfully placed, accent curves in the path.

OPPOSITE: The slightly undulating form of a bridge repeats the shape of the serpentine wall seen in the distance. Here, the hard gray of the stone walls, bridge, and walkway are in sharp contrast to the rich colors of the surrounding landscape. In the foreground are twin Japanese maples—one red, the other an intense yellow. Venerable yews make striking vertical statements and seem to serve as sentries for the path as it wanders away from the house.

OPPOSITE: In winter, the "bones" of the garden are revealed when flowers and deciduous foliage disappear. Paths and paved areas—along with walls, fences, hedges, and lawns—form the framework of the garden's basic structure. In this winter garden, a brick path is interrupted by a flagstone circle adorned with an armillary sphere. Surrounding the flagstone disk are concentric circles of lawn and planting beds designed to emphasize the central ornament.

RIGHT: A hard-packed path of bare earth winds through an enchanting early-spring scene of snowdrops in full bloom. The simplicity of the path is perfectly in sync with the natural setting of ethereal bulbs, new grass, and a twig fence hidden among the trees.

BELOW: A grass path is barely discernible as it passes through a spring garden carpeted with forget-me-nots and dotted with tulips. Eventually the path leaves the open space of the garden and winds its way through the frothy mass of white dogwoods.

ABOVE: The zigzag of a slender brick path makes its way through a ribbon of a border thickly planted with variegated hostas, artemisia, pink yarrow and cosmos, and a mass of white nicotiana. The brick element is repeated in the edging of the pond behind the hostas.

ABOVE: In an old walled garden, herbs grow in triangular beds established by weathered bricks set in an unusual pattern. Surrounding these triangles are pale rectangular stones set end to end to create a perimeter walkway that is in turn framed by dense plantings of chives in full bloom.

ABOVE: Large pavers in two tones of gray are arranged in a modified basketweave pattern in the Barnsley House potager. The intersection of the narrow paths is surrounded by a subtle circle of red bricks. Within the circle are variegated strawberries, fruit trees, and four rounded boxwoods.

ABOVE: Crazy paving in York stone edged with brick forms a wide and dramatic path that follows the contours of a fast-moving stream. The swathe of soft green lawn, the dark and glistening water, the canopy of pale green willow, and the lighter tones and rougher surface of the bricks and stones form a complex arrangement of colors, shapes, and textures.

RIGHT: A melange of textures, colors, and shapes create a visually stimulating alternative to paving in this former driveway. Pea gravel, irregular stepping stones, and serpentine brick lines define a path to the door, while the rest of the gravel serves as an alternative to lawn, mulch, or more typical planting beds.

BELOW: Rough gravel is used here to create paths among raised beds, but the walkway is all but hidden by vigorous plantings. In gardens near the sea, crushed shells or coarse sand often serve the same function as gravel.

Chapter Two

THE BEGINNING AND THE END

*W*here to start? How to end? These are important questions for the gardener faced with the task of designing and installing a garden path. Some paths do evolve naturally. For example, in a small backyard, the most comfortable route from back door to garage, garden shed, or vegetable beds soon becomes evident as the lawn becomes worn. A natural path in a woodland or meadow or along a stream becomes apparent when people regularly walk there. In these instances, it's best to follow the most obvious course and construct the path along that route.

However, in the case of a new or reworked design, one might put down paths anywhere. That having been said, it's always best to create a garden path that actually serves a purpose. The intention may be to physically move the gardener or visitor from one place to another, or it may be to motivate a visual journey through the garden.

Whatever the raison d'etre of the path, it is sure to benefit from a distinct beginning and end, unless you are planning a circular walk. Paths that seem to appear out of nowhere and end at a fence or hedge are disquieting to the spirit— they simply don't look natural. One practical beginning or end to any path is at a door or a gate; if the path is to begin at a point away from the door, say, after an area of lawn but before the garden proper, a portal may be created with a hedge or an arbor.

Giving a path a defined end point creates a sense of anticipation and draws the visitor forward through the garden. A gazebo, summer house, and simple bench are all places of respite that offer ample reward for traveling the path. A grand vista or an expertly placed focal point, such as a piece of sculpture or an ornamental birdbath, are also fine terminal points.

No matter what the material, plantings, or layout of the path, giving careful thought to the start and end of the route will almost guarantee a successful path design.

OPPOSITE: The view from one end of this wide grass path to the grotto that forms its far vista is beautifully interrupted by the glorious and varied plantings. The three connected fountains that traverse the path's center offer a visual rest stop for the viewer's eye, which may otherwise find the richness of this display a little overwhelming.

RIGHT: The classic geometry of straight lines and circles is especially successful along this box-edged path. A mammoth urn, with its towering cordyline, makes a dramatic focal point in the center of the circle. If an urn is not to your taste, a fountain, statue, or a graceful Japanese maple would do nicely too.

ABOVE: The arched gate at the end of this grass avenue adds mystery and surprise to a garden scheme. This scene is further enhanced by an enormous rose in full bloom, which will soon litter the grass with its fallen petals.

OPPOSITE: The round "Moon Gate" at Greencombe Garden in Somerset leads the visitor up a short flight of steps into a vegetable garden. An unexpected shape like this round entrance is at once jarring and exciting. The ordinary brick path in the vegetable garden beyond the gate supplies a reassuring return to the expected, while its running bond pattern pulls the visitor through the gate and into the garden.

ABOVE LEFT: A contemporary sculpture is the visual reward at the end of narrow grass path that is marked at both its beginning and its end by thick, arched hedges. Twin borders in monochromatic green offer little distraction along the way.

ABOVE RIGHT: A stone-paved path with several steps passes through an arched "door" in a yew hedge—this hedge serves as a marker between the kitchen garden and the pool garden. The path ends at the lawn of the adjoining garden room, but the vista carries further, terminating at the graceful bench guarded by rugosa roses on the far side of the pool.

OPPOSITE: In a tiny garden space, order is maintained amid a clutter of blooms. The organizing theme is a simple gravel path dotted with square and round pavers. Along its short span, the path reaches out to form pockets within the planting areas. The end of the path is quietly noted by a rabbit and a dove.

ABOVE: Thickly laid crushed white stone forms a path around a stone-edged pool and waterfall. The bamboo lattice gate seems to float above the gravel, but is anchored by the Japanese maple nearby. Short wooden posts set at varying heights along the path keep the beds well contained and add a formal yet natural-looking element to the design.

OPPOSITE: Decorative iron gates lead into and out of this walled Irish garden, linked by a simple gravel path. Beyond the second gate, a flight of stone steps leads to yet another portal—this one in a stone wall—that opens onto a sun-filled space beyond the confines of the garden. The simplicity of the straight gravel path is in marked contrast to the intricate curves of the ornate gates.

ABOVE: Despite the visual demands of a vividly planted garden, the eye remains drawn to the elegant gazebo that forms the terminus of this stone-edged grass path. Without a strong focal point, the path, which is somewhat narrow given the width of the adjacent beds, might have become overwhelmed by the intensity of the plantings.

OPPOSITE: A charming statue, framed by the metal form of an arbor, marks the point where brick paths form a junction. Though the tangle of purple and pink clematis and climbing roses require attention, the walkways' divergent paths have strong visual interest and one can't help but be curious about what lies to the right or the left.

ABOVE: A modest front garden is given a boost by the playful placement of paving stones in the lawn. The steps leading down to the lawn are perfectly conventional, making the scattered stone path that much more whimsical.

LEFT: In this charming southern garden, a running bond pattern of bricks, which tends to draw the eye along, curves past a bed of 'Stella d'Oro' daylilies to a series of terminal points. The first is a doorway, the second a peacock-style iron chair, and the final ending is a patio area. Because the path is simple and the plantings uncomplicated, the multitude of terminal points does not unduly jar the eye.

OPPOSITE: There's more than a hint of the Orient in this Texas garden, where a vividly painted pagoda-like garden house overlooks a small pond. Surrounding the pond is a narrow gravel walkway that is in turn enclosed within a cobblestone path. A Chippendale-style bench is perched serenely atop the cobblestones, becoming a focal point in a garden with many elements successfully competing for attention.

ABOVE: A pair of ivy topiary birds flanking a graceful white metal bench sit at the end of one path and along the route of another that forms the top of a T. The white bench together with ivory and silver plantings create a polished vignette.

OPPOSITE: The beauty and elegance of this lichen-encrusted stone walk with its edging of cobbles is accentuated by the simple lines of a classic wooden bench. Artfully set at an angle where the path turns a corner, the bench is further integrated into the garden by the addition of several lushly planted terra-cotta pots. Though the bench is a focal point and the plantings are grand, with its rich textures and handsome patterns the walkway is the true star of this show.

Chapter Three

MATERIALS FOR PATHS AND WALKWAYS

*W*hile paths and walkways may be made from many different materials, there are three basic categories—organic materials like grass and wood; stone in all its various shapes and forms; and man-made products like bricks, tiles, and concrete pavers.

The diversity of materials available offers gardeners a wide range of choices in color, texture, shape, pattern, durability, and price. Bricks, for example, are made from many types of clay or concrete, with colors running from nearly white to dark blue to blackish and speckled. They can be wire cut or pressed, brand new or aged, handmade and distinctive, or mass-produced and completely uniform. Other man-made materials used to create paths and walkways include concrete pavers in round, hexagonal, square, rectangular, or interlocking shapes; aggregate concrete paving slabs of varying textures; artificial stone paving blocks; poured and tinted concrete paving units; terra-cotta tiles; and glazed accent tiles.

Stone offers even more variety in its appearance and in the way it is used. Large, flat limestone, sandstone, Pennsylvania bluestone, and slate slabs are mined in quarries and often cut into squares or rectangles for paths of many descriptions. Stepping stones or crazy paving patterns can be created from broken, irregular pieces of flat stone, while round or oval egg-sized cobbles are used loose or set in mortar for highly textured walkways. In the nineteenth century hard granite blocks were used to pave streets, and today they are incorporated into paths as the paving surface or as edging. Walkways and paths can also be constructed of smaller stones in the form of gravel, which is available in shades of gray, white, pink, black, and beige. Gravel is also sold in various sizes ranging from fine grit to chips to coarse pebbles.

The third class of materials for paths and walkways are the organic things—grass, hard-packed earth, and wood. Wood takes many forms, including chips and shredded bark, cut rounds of tree trunks used for stepping "stone" paths, rough-sawn planks, and smooth finished decking for boardwalks and bridges. Grass and earth are perhaps the simplest of materials, requiring only slight participation from the gardener—periodic mowing or the treading action of regular traffic are the only construction techniques necessary for grass and dirt paths.

While the diversity of these fundamental materials is vast, it is in the interpretation of their use that we see the wealth of variety and creativity that gardeners bring to the design of paths and walkways.

OPPOSITE: A complex design calls for innovative use of materials. In this creative garden, square terra-cotta tiles are grouped in fours to build larger squares. These squares are then set on the diagonal to form a vertical line of connected diamond shapes. The neatly clipped chevron shapes of the low boxwood hedges intensify the striking visual effect.

ABOVE LEFT: Large and uniformly, though naturally, shaped stepping stones are evenly spaced to form a welcoming path through a small garden space. Paths like this are designed to allow the gardener access to planting areas. A curve in the path adds a sense of mystery and surprise, and the narrow width invites a contemplative walk on one's own.

ABOVE RIGHT: A loosely spaced double row of large bricks in a simple basket-weave pattern—two up, two across—has been used in the construction of this narrow vegetable garden path. However, the two types of brick— narrow red ones and wider gray pavers—create a truly dynamic play of color and texture, which is accentuated by the rows of tiny boxwood on either side of the path.

OPPOSITE: Made shiny by the rain, irregular river stones are carefully set between cobblestones to create a lively entrance path. Such a path, with its unusual combination of textures, works well with the green living walls that surround it.

ABOVE: In this pretty spring scene, a path of gray and buff-colored gravel is little more than a narrow divide between beds of winter aconite, hellebores, and snowdrops. Here the stone is allowed to flow unrestrained by edging into the beds, blurring the line between path and plantings. In this setting, a mulch path would be equally effective, whereas a grass path might lessen the impact.

RIGHT: Contemporary landscape schemes require a studied hand in the selection and placement of materials. Here, a series of graded steps to a wide brick landing are constructed with railroad ties, mixed gravel, and concrete pavers. The sprawling juniper and delicate daisies on the right soften the hard-edged composition, while the clipped boxwood globes add a note of formality.

OPPOSITE: In this unusual display, a ring of large, rounded pebbles set in mortar and edged with stone blocks encloses a round gravel garden of low-growing grasses and alpine plants. The circular theme is repeated in the slightly raised stone dining area and in the forms of the marble-topped tables. While enormously successful in this stunning garden, using too many distinctive materials can result in an overly busy design.

ABOVE: This contemporary design incorporates four materials—oversized rectangular brick pavers, square-cut stones, wood cylinders, and dark wood mulch—for an austere walkway and landscape bed. The key to a successful path is matching the materials and the form to the landscape theme and the surrounding structures.

LEFT: A thick new layer of hardwood mulch forms a naturalistic path through feathery clumps of purple larkspur. The mulch looks best when allowed to drift off into the beds. Here, a clump of irises actually grows up in the path, adding to the appeal of the garden. Mulch and wood chips are among the simplest materials to use for making paths, and are especially suitable for woodland trails and country gardens. They do eventually break down as the material decomposes and must be restored with a new application every year or so.

ABOVE: In a naturalized hillside setting, the irregular shapes of log slices create an unobtrusive walkway among the hostas, ligularia, and rodgersia. Natural stone steps, as opposed to cut stone, would be another appropriate choice. But imagine bricks, concrete, or cobblestones instead and the scene changes from serene to awkward and disruptive.

ABOVE: A swirl of reddish broken flagstones circles a pair of trees to create a showcase for spectacular miniature narcissi and multicolored double tulips. Large stands of tulips, narcissi, and fritillaria form a spectacular ring of bloom outside the circle.

LEFT: Thousands of tiny daisies carpet a grass path in a country setting. Though ephemeral—they don't linger for long—their cheerful presence is eagerly awaited each year. As the flowers fade, the uncomplicated path will return to its simple green wardrobe.

OPPOSITE: Areas of azaleas, camellias, rhododendrons, and magnolias are linked by carefully edged grass paths in this peaceful woodland garden. Though the garden is delightfully natural, vigilant effort is needed to maintain the sharp path edges that set off the color and form of the abundant plantings.

LEFT: Vivid blue tiles, used sparingly within an irregular brick walk, create the happy impression of a crazy quilt thrown down beside a bed of delicate flowers. This charming early-spring vignette includes 'Pippit' narcissus, forget-me-nots, and the feathery foliage of love-in-a-mist in bud. When the love-in-a-mist blooms, its pale blue flowers will harmonize beautifully with the stronger blue of the handmade tiles.

OPPOSITE: An ordinary flight of brick steps becomes a stage for an elaborate show of blooms and foliage including peonies, foxgloves, euphorbia, and diminutive daisies. Evergreen plantings hold the scene together when the perennials retreat for the winter.

BELOW: Crosshatched stable bricks lend visual spice to what could be an ordinary front path. Instead, the bricks add texture and form with a pleasing contrast to the smoother qualities of the railroad tie steps and walkway. These bricks were traditionally used in stables because they provide a good footing in slippery conditions. The entrance here is made all the more inviting by well-chosen plantings, including plenty of cottage-style plants that spill endearingly onto the walk.

Chapter Four

PLANTS FOR EDGING PATHS AND WALKWAYS

For any given place in the garden, there are often dozens of appropriate and pleasing plant choices. What plants one finally selects often has more to do with taste and preference than specific garden design rules.

Of course, that is not to say that anything can go anywhere!

The first consideration in choosing plants is to understand their needs: do they require sun or shade? Moist or dry conditions? Humus or sandy soil? Are they hardy or tender? By selecting plants that thrive in the conditions in which they are planted, success is all but guaranteed.

Secondly, one must think about size and shape. It won't do to plant towering perennials under a low shrub. And it's equally inappropriate to plant masses of low-growing things when vertical interest is needed. But creeping varieties, like thyme or sedums, are delightful when planted in the spaces between stones in a cottage garden walkway. And tall plants, like lupines or delphiniums, are perfectly at home at the edge of a wide grass path.

Color is another vital consideration, and here the choices are enormously wide-ranging. An all-white garden along a red brick path or hot color borders of reds, oranges, and yellows divided by a cool gray stone walk are completely different treatments, yet both are equally arresting. Or perhaps a garden of pink and lavender transversed by a vibrant green grass path is more to your taste. A no-holds-barred array of every shade imaginable is still another option, and there's always the elegance of a foliage garden that celebrates the variety and range of the color green.

Texture is also significant. Wispy ornamental grasses, feathery fennel, or frothy dianthus can soften the harsh edges of a too-new brick walkway. Soft, fuzzy plants like lamb's ears or mullein make a strong contrast with the leathery leaves of bergenia or the quilted ones of hostas. When distinctive textures—

including the textures of the paths themselves—are artfully mixed, the resulting garden is full of interest and complexity.

And of course, among the most important considerations when selecting plants for one's own garden is to use the plants you love the most—so that each time you venture down the garden path, you are reunited with old friends.

ABOVE: On both sides of a rustic stone path, a bold display of old-fashioned annuals luxuriates in the setting sun. Competing for attention are spider flowers (*Cleome*), marigolds, zinnias, salvia, and sunflowers, while quieter clumps of white sweet alyssum ingratiate themselves between the stones. Encouraging plants to grow in the irregular spaces between stones is especially appropriate in country-style gardens.

OPPOSITE: Few sights are as refreshing as that of a hillside blanketed by naturalized daffodils. Here, the cheerful faces of the daffs face a well-worn and unpretentious dirt track.

ABOVE: An eye-popping collection of asters in warm shades of pink, rose, red, and white is set against the backdrop of a gorgeous copper beech hedge. But despite the star quality of these potential competitors, the eye naturally seeks a more soothing sight and is drawn to the green grass path as it curves out of sight.

OPPOSITE: A grass path through a wooded garden is especially magical when the rhododendrons bloom. This majestic example, 'Pink Diamond', towers over the path, forcing visitors to stop and stare. Later, the strong shapes of the rhododendron shrubs will form an attractive green wall along the path, but other plantings will claim primary attention.

ABOVE: Two old-fashioned favorites—red salvia and silver dusty miller—make an unusually strong statement when lining a path of gray crazy paving. The deep green of the grape vine clinging to the brick wall and the bright green of the grass alongside the path keep the composition from becoming too loud.

RIGHT: A natural stone path offers a different perspective when it curves out of sight, adding a sense of mystery or surprise. And here, instead of flashy annuals, is a collection of perennials guarded by a fine blue spruce. Refusing to remain within their beds are gooseneck loosestrife, ajuga, variegated hostas, and bright yellow coreopsis 'Golden Showers'.

OPPOSITE: A Classical statue at the end of this icy grass path is eerily lifelike in the winter air. The huge clumps of perennials flanking the path were left intact long after their blooms were spent. Though lifeless, the dried forms maintain a stately presence in the dormant garden.

ABOVE: Fiery red hot poker (*Kniphofia*) takes center stage at the edge of a lichen-covered stone path. Masses of yellow daisylike *Bupthalmum* and tall, red Maltese cross are lively supporting actors in this hot color border. Hot color gardens, a concept perfected by legendary garden designer Gertrude Jekyll, generally avoid the cooler tones of lemon yellows and bluish-reds in favor of the warmer shades of gold and orange-red.

RIGHT: On either side of a narrow gravel path, big lush beds seem to explode with yellow blooms. Roses, lupines, yarrow, coreopsis, lady's mantle, foxtail lilies, and daisies are all in bloom at once. The unpretentious simplicity of the path accentuates the garden's nearly untamed look. Imagine how changed the garden would be if the beds were separated by a wide grass path edged in cut stone blocks.

ABOVE: Ball-on-ball boxwood topiaries cast nearly human shadows on a beautifully designed brick walkway in this formal *potager*. The lavender edging running the length of the path accentuates the path's pattern, which, with its march of gray center blocks, directs the viewer's glance to the arbor of 'Rambling Rector' roses at the path's end.

OPPOSITE: In this primarily green garden, the grass path is carefully edged and lined with a repetitive row of plants, encouraging the eye to hurry to the focal point—an unusual octagonal hedge of clipped bush-form honeysuckle. The work of an artistic hand is evident here in the wonderful blending and harmonizing of shades of green. Note how the bright green of the grass path is set off by the blue-green edging material. Darker greens among the evergreens add to the complexity of the composition.

ABOVE: A simple, sturdy, and utilitarian flagstone path plays a supporting role to the plantings in the forecourt at Sissinghurst Castle, where massive and ancient climbing roses, pale irises, and a collection of plants in pots and old stone sinks receive the admiring glances of visitors.

RIGHT: Sprawling lady's mantle in a froth of unrestrained chartreuse along a brick path compete for attention with deep pink roses trained along rope swags. Holding the middle ground are pink shrub roses and large plantings of lavender.

ABOVE: The gray shades of a chipped-stone path and the stone edging bordering the lawn and pond are a unifying agent for a busy and colorful garden. In a garden with an eclectic and broad collection of elements—color, texture, shape, size, form—competing for attention, a simple link, like the gray stone, is essential in order to avoid visual anarchy.

ABOVE: Here is a garden where plant textures and shapes have been cleverly combined to create interesting associations. Tall tufts of feather grass and its shorter relatives are lively companions to the low-growing mounds of white rock rose and the soft, feathery leaves of gray-green mullein. The buff-colored pea gravel path that winds its way through the garden and insinuates itself among the plants is a unifying force among these diverse textures and shapes.

LEFT: Thick double borders line a bleached wood boardwalk. Among the densely planted varieties are lilies, astilbe, gooseneck loosestrife, and lady's mantle. While flowers planted this close together may need dividing more often, weeds will have less of an opportunity to get a root hold.

Index

INDEX

Aconite, 51, *51*
Ajuga, 63, *63*
Allee, 19, *19*
Allium, 6, *7*
Artemisia, 10, *10*, 28, *28*
Aster, 60, *60*
Astilbe, 70–71, *71*
Azaleas, 23, *23*, 54, *55*

Boxwood, 13, *13*, 23, *23*, 33, *33*, 46, 47, 48, *48*, 51, *51*, 67, *67*
Brick, 10, *10*, *18–19*, *19*, 26, 27, 28, *28*, 29, *29*, 30, *30*, 31, *31*, 34, *34*, 40, 41, 42, *42*, 48, *48*, 52, *52*, 56, *56*, 57, 67, *67*

Camellias, 54, *55*
Catmint 13, *13*, 14
Ceramic tile, 56, *56*
Chamomile, 14, *15*
Chives, 28, *28*
Clematis, 40, *41*
Cobbles, 6, *7*, 42, *43*, *44*, *45*, *48*, *49*
Concrete pavers, 29, *29*, 37, *37*, 51, *51*
Coreopsis, 63, *63*, 64, *64–65*
Cosmos, 28, *28*

Daffodils, 58, *59*
Daisies, 51, *51*, 55, *55*, 56, 57, 64, *64–65*
Daylilies, 14, 42, *42*
Delphiniums, 16, *17*
Dusty miller, 63, *63*

Euphorbia, 56, *57*

Ferns, 23, *23*, 24, *24*
Forget-me-nots, 27, *27*, 56, *56*
Foxglove, 56, *57*
Foxtail lilies, 64, *64–65*
Fritillaria, 55, *55*

Geraniums, 14, *14*
Gooseneck loosestrife, 63, *63*, 70–71, *71*
Gravel, 10, *10*, *13*, 13, 22, 23, *23*, 24, *24*, 31, *31*, 37, *37*, 38, *39*, 42, *43*, 51, *51*, 64, *64–65*, 70–71, *71*

Hellebores, 51, *51*
Honeysuckle, 66, *67*
Hornbeam, 19, *19*, 20, *21*
Hosta, 24, *24*, 28, *28*, 63, *63*

Iris, 8, *9*, 10, *10*, 14, *15*, 24, *24*, 52, *52*, 68, *68*

Japanese maple, 24, *25*, 38, *38*
Juniper, 51, *51*

Lady's mantle, 14, 16, *17*, 64, *64–65*, 68, *68*
Lamb's ears, 23, *23*
Larkspur, 52, *52*
Lavender, 10, *10*, 14, *14*, 67, *67*, 68, *68*
Lilies, 70–71, *71*
Lilyturf, *12*, 13
Love-in-a-mist, 56, *56*
Lupine, 64, *64–65*,

Maltese cross, 64, *64*
Marigolds, 59, *59*
Mulch, 52, *52*
Mullein, 70–71, *71*

Narcissus, 55, *55*, 56, *56*

Path materials
  brick, 10, *10*, *18–19*, *19*, 26, 27, 28, *28*, 29, *29*, 30, *30*, 31, *31*, 34, *34*, 40, 41, 42, *42*, 48, *48*, 52, *52*, 67, *67*
  ceramic tile, 56, *56*,
  cobbles, 6, *7*, 42, *43*, *44*, *45*, *48*, *49*
  concrete pavers, 29, *29*, 37, *37*, 51, *51*
  earth, 27, *27*, 58, *59*
  grass, 16, *16*, *17*, 19, *19*, 20, 21, 23, *23*, 27, 27, 32, 33, 34, *34*, 37, *37*, 41, *41*, 55, *55*, 60, *60*, *61*, *62*, 63, *66*, *67*
  gravel, 10, *10*, *13*, *13*, 23, 23, 24, *24*, 31, *31*, 37, *37*, 38, *39*, 42, *43*, 51, *51*, 64, *64–65*, 70–71, *71*
  mulch, 52, *52*
  stone, 6, *7*, 9, *9*, 10, *10*, 24, *25*, 28, *28*, 30, *30*, 31, *31*, 37, *37*, 41, *41*, 42, *42*, *44*, *45*, 48, *48*, 49, *50*, 51, 52, *52*, 55, *55*, 59, *59*, 63, *63*, 64, *64*, 68, *68*, 69, *69*
  pebbles, *12*, 13, 50, 51
  terra-cotta tiles, *46*, 47
  wood, 24, *24*, 53, *53*, 70–71, *71*
Pebbles, *12*, 13, 50, 51
Peony, 56, *57*

Railroad ties, 51, *51*, 56, *56*
Red hot poker, 64, *64*
Rhododendron, 23, *23*, 54, 55, 60, *61*
Rock rose, 70–71, *71*

'Rose du Mai' dianthus, 13, *13*
Rose, 16, *17*, 34, *34*, 37, *37*, 40, 41, 64, *64–65*, 67, *67*, 68, *68*

Sage, 14, *14*
Salvia, 59, *59*, 63, *63*
Snowdrops, 27, *27*, 51, *51*
Spider flowers, 59, *59*
Stepping stones, 48, *48*
Stocks, 10, *10*
Stone, 6, *7*, 9, *9*, 10, *10*, 24, *25*, 28, *28*, 30, *30*, 31, *31*, 37, *37*, 41, *41*, 42, *42*, *44*, 45, 48, *49*, 50, 51, 52, *52*, 55, *55*, 59, *59*, 63, *63*, 64, *64*, 68, *68*, 69, *69*
Sunflowers, 59, *59*
Sweet alyssum, 59, *59*

Terra-cotta tiles, *46*, 47
Tulips, 27, *27*, 55, *55*

Yarrow, *18–19*, 19, 28, *28*, 64, *64–65*
Yew, 24, *25*, 37, *37*

Zinnia, 59, *59*

PHOTO CREDITS

©Daria Bowman: 68 top

©Derek Fell: 8, 12, 24 bottom, 27 bottom, 49, 59

©John Glover: 18-19, 22, 28 left, 36, 37 both, 40, 41, 46, 55 left, 64-65

©Dency Kane: 70-71

©Clive Nichols: 6, 29, 48 right (Barnsley House, Gloucestershire); 9 (designed by Anne Dexter); 10 left, 71 right (designed by Mark Brown); 10-11, 34 (Wollerton Old Hall, Shropshire); 13 (The Anchorage, Kent); 14 (Sticky Wicket, Dorset); 15 (The Garden House, Gloucestershire); 16 (Great Dixter, Sussex); 17, 67 (Old Rectory, Northamptonshire); 19 right, 20 (designed by David Hicks); 23 left (Cartier/Harpers & Queen Garden, Chelsea, 1994, designed by Mark Walker); 23 right, 53 (designed by Anne Waring); 24 top (The Hannah Peschar Gallery Garden, Surrey); 25 (Dinmore Manor, Hereford & Worcester); 26 (designed by Roy Strong); 27 top (Benington Lordship, Hertfordshire); 28 right; 30 (Mrs. Styles' Garden, Oxon); 31 top (designed by Fearnley-Whittingstall); 2, 31 bottom, 33, 56 right (Turn End Garden, Bucks); 32 (The Telegraph Garden, Chelsea, 1995, designed by A. Lennox-Boyd); 35 (Greencombe Garden, Somerset); 38 (Honda Tea Garden, Chelsea, 1995, Designed by Julian Dowle & K. Ninomiya); 39 (Butterstream Garden, Republic of Ireland); 42 right (designed by Christopher Masson); 43 (designed by Gordon White); 45 (Chenies Manor, Bucks); 48 left, 69 (The Crossing House, Hertfordshire); 50 (Evening Standard Garden, Chelsea, 1995, designed by Julie Toll); 51 bottom (designed by Jill Billington); 51 top, 62 (The Old Rectory, Berkshire); 52 right (Save the Children/EMI Garden, Chelsea, 1991); 54 (Ramster Woodland Garden, Surrey); 55 right (Keukenhof Gardens, Holland); 56 left (designed by Keeyla Meadows); 57 (designed by John Plummer, Chelsea, 1993); 58 (Weir Gardens, Hereford & Worcester); 60 (Picton Garden, Worcestershire); 61 (Ramster Garden, Surrey); 63 left (Ian McArthur's Garden, Reading); 64 left (The Manor House, Upton Grey, Hampshire); 66 (Osler RD, Oxford); 68 bottom (Mrs. Glaisher's Garden, Kent)

©Jerry Pavia: 44, 52 left, 63 right

Photo/Nats, Inc.: ©Gay Bumgarner: 42 left